HAVE A LITTLE PUN

HAVE A LITTLE PUN

AN ILLUSTRATED PLAY ON WORDS

BY FRIDA CLEMENTS

CHRONICLE BOOKS
SAN FRANCISCO

LIBRARY OF CONGRESS CATALOGING-IN-PUBLICATION DATA AVAILABLE.

ISBN 978-1-4521-4416-0

MANUFACTURED IN CHINA

ILLUSTRATIONS AND LETTERING BY FRIDA CLEMENTS.

LAYOUT BY HILLARY CAUDLE.

10 9 8 7 6 5 4 3 2 1

CHRONICLE BOOKS LLC
680 SECOND STREET
SAN FRANCISCO, CALIFORNIA 94107

www.chroniclebooks.com

"*Puns are the highest form of literature.*"
— *Alfred Hitchcock*

"I think puns are not just the lowest form
of wit, but the lowest form of human behavior.
The moment that I accept that there's an
artistic, redeeming quality in puns,
I have a horrible feeling I'll get hooked."
— John Oliver

"I LIVE AND DIE BY PUNS"
— FEIST

INTRODUCTION

I think I've always enjoyed a good pun. When my dear husband and I were just newlyweds (and cleaning out the fridge), I said to him, "That dill is done. It's a done dill." I then doubled over with laughter, while he quietly pondered what was wrong with me. Little did we know that I had "found my porpoise."

My impulse to put pun to paper began on a rainy night at a Seattle pub, where I had been invited to a sketch meet-up of local artists. I arrived, pen and paper in hand, excited to draw . . . and it was a ghost town. I had mixed up the date. There is solace in knowing that most creative people struggle with the details of everyday life, like writing things down in calendars. And I am definitely one of those people.

Once I returned home that evening, I decided that there was no reason I couldn't just sketch for fun anyway. So I drew a whale. I looked at that whale. I thought about my random brain that can't keep anything straight and hand-lettered OH WHALE in all caps under my drawing. From that moment on, the puns took over.

Now the puns flow faster than I can commit them to paper, mostly inspired by everyday moments and conversations. "Birch Please" happened while driving past some birch trees on the way to my daughter's school. "Oh My Cod" was scrawled on a receipt for fish tacos. I keep a running list on my nightstand and have been known to shake my husband awake and excitedly whisper stuff like, "MAUL about that! With a BEAR! Get it?" One of the funniest ideas, however, came via text message from my sister-in-law. She is an elementary school teacher. It simply read, "For Fox Sake."

I hope this book brings a smile, giggle, grin, or groan, and even a little daily inspiration, so that if your day is cray cray you can just say, Oh whale. That's coo.

What the hail, have a little pun!

GOPHER IT

QUITE FAWNED OF YOU

HONEY BEE YOURSELF

FIND YOUR.
PORPOISE

EWE CRAZY

IT'S MEOW
OR NEVER

I KID

MAUL
ABOUT
THAT

DILL WITH IT

WHY SO CRABBY

ROLL WITH IT

I'LL BE DAMMED

FUR SURE

PRETTY FLY

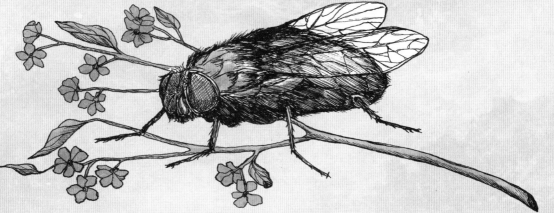

A·LITTLE ANTSY

KNOTTY ⋆ KNOTTY

OH WHALE

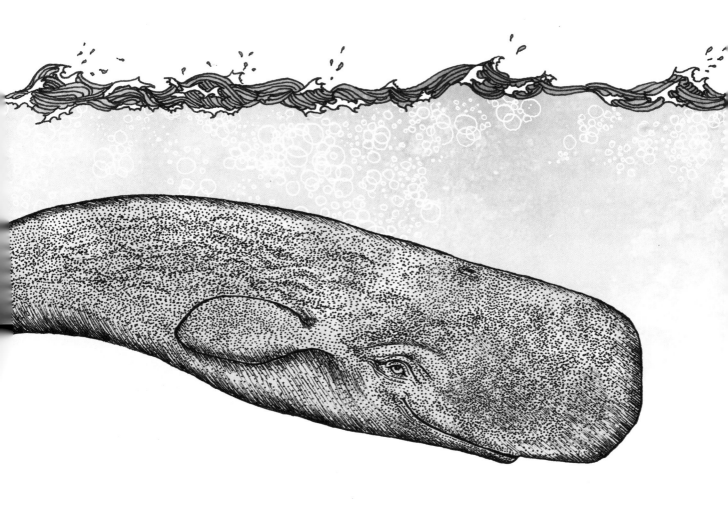

TOTAL BULL

MURDER ONE

RIGHT ON THYME

BAD
HARE
DAY

CRAY CRAY

BIRCH
PLEASE

DON'T CARROT ALL

NICE MUSSELS

OH MY COD

THAT'S
COO

MOSS DEF

ROCK ON

PEONIES
ENVY

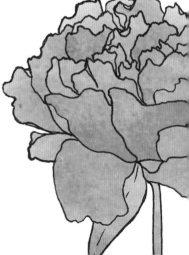

WHY I OTTER.

MAKE IT
SNAP PEA

ONCE A CHEETAH ALWAYS A CHEETAH

KNOCK
ON
WOOD

THAT'S MY JAM

ACKNOWLEDGMENTS

THANK YOU TOMO NAKAYAMA – MY PARTNER IN LIFE AND IN ART. THIS BOOK WOULDN'T HAVE BEEN POSSIBLE WITHOUT THE SUPPORT OF THESE INCREDIBLE PEOPLE: MARDI CLEMENTS AND DAVID ALLEN; THE NAKAYAMA-TRAN CLAN; THE MELANDER FAMILY; BILL, MATT, AND ASHLEY CLEMENTS; BRIAN ALLEN; TES DELUNA; AMY HEVRON; HEIDI HOLMQUIST; DEEP DASGUPTA; LAUREN DANIELS; AMANDA BEDELL; ROBYNNE RAYE; ADAM ZACKS AND LYNN RESNICK; ADAM MacKINNON; AND MY TWO AMAZING KIDS, FOREST AND SAGE. FINALLY, MASSIVE HEARTFELT GRATITUDE TO STEVE MOCKUS AT CHRONICLE BOOKS FOR TOTALLY GETTING IT RIGHT AWAY AND BEING THE COOLEST EDITOR THAT PROBABLY EVER EXISTED.

FOR SAGE, THE FUNNIEST AND WISEST GIRL I KNOW.
GLAD WE HAVE SO MUCH PUN TOGETHER.

ABOUT THE AUTHOR

Frida Clements is a Seattle-based illustrator and graphic designer particularly known for her beautiful screen-printed music, theater, and art poster designs. She's probably thinking of another pun right now. See more of her work at fridaclements.com.